Three bouncing balls—
one red, one green, one blue—

slipped off a toy shelf
and got kicked by a shoe.

They bounced out the door
and down a dozen steps.

They bounced past the postman
and Mrs. Cadoodle's pets.

They bounced into a wagon
and the three, they took a ride—

5

bump, bump, bump to the playground,
where they slid down a slippery slide.

Next, they bounced beside a singer
and a very silly clown,

who scooped them all up—one, two, three!—
and juggled them round and round.

Then, he dropped them in a fountain
where those three balls had a bath.

Then squeaky clean, they bounced, bounced, bounced along a garden path.

After that, they were super-sleepy,
so the little red ball said,

"One, two, three, let's roll right home

and bounce into our bed."

three balls, three trucks, three teddy bears
and three dinosaurs in three little chairs?

What other sets of three do you see?

## Hooray for Three!

Let's clap three times
and touch the ground.
Let's jump three times
and spin around.
Let's stomp three times
and cheer and shout
for a wonderful number
we can't live without:
THREE!